Jacob Mortimer Wier Silver

Sketches of Japanese Manners and Customs

Jacob Mortimer Wier Silver

Sketches of Japanese Manners and Customs

ISBN/EAN: 9783337167851

Printed in Europe, USA, Canada, Australia, Japan

Cover: Foto ©Thomas Meinert / pixelio.de

More available books at **www.hansebooks.com**

SKETCHES

OF

JAPANESE MANNERS AND CUSTOMS.

BY

J. M. W. SILVER,

LIEUTENANT ROYAL MARINES, LIGHT INFANTRY.

(LATE OF THE ROYAL MARINE BATTALION FOR SERVICE IN JAPAN.)

Illustrated by Native Drawings,

REPRODUCED IN FAC-SIMILE BY MEANS OF CHROMO-LITHOGRAPHY

LONDON:

DAY AND SON, LIMITED.

Lithographers and Publishers,

6, GATE STREET, LINCOLN'S INN FIELDS, W.C.

1867.

TO

COLONEL SIR EDMUND SAUNDERSON PRIDEAUX,
BART.

DEAR SIR EDMUND,

These few 'Sketches of Japanese Manners and Customs' were collected during the years 1864–5, at which time I was attached to the Battalion of Royal Marines for service in Japan, and it is now very pleasing to have the privilege of dedicating them to one who was the friend and companion-in-arms of my late Father.

In memory of this bond of friendship, and in grateful acknowledgment of the many kindnesses you have shown me, this Dedication of my humble efforts to assist in the elucidation of the social condition of a distant and comparatively unknown race, affords me deep gratification.

With much respect and esteem, I am,

Dear Sir Edmund,

Very faithfully yours,

J. M. W. SILVER.

Royal Marine Barracks, Forton.
January 29th, 1867.

470399

CONTENTS.

LIST OF PLATES.

ERRATA.

In Page 2, after 'crimson streamers,' there should be a semicolon.

8, *for* 'Yokahama,' *read* 'Yokohama.'

Note, page 9, *for* 'the people,' *read* 'they.'

JAPANESE MANNERS AND CUSTOMS.

CHAPTER I.

FESTIVALS AND HOLIDAYS.

THE first feature of Japanese life that prominently presents itself to the notice of the stranger, is the number of festivals and holidays held in honour of the various deities, warriors, and sages, or in accordance with some ancient custom of the country, which is as paramount an authority as the most stringent of its laws. Of these festivals, the 'Oki-don-tako,' or 'Great Holiday,' which takes place about Christmas, and lasts a fortnight, is the most important. Previous to its celebration, it is customary with the people to settle accounts, and amicably adjust any quarrels or estrangements that may happen to exist; and they evince the same spirit that actuates Christian nations at this season, by a general interchange of presents and complimentary visits with their friends and acquaintance. So anxious are the merchants to take this opportunity of settling with their creditors, that, when the dealers have deficiencies to make up, articles are frequently pressed on foreign residents at the Treaty Ports at prices previously refused.

The 'Gogats Seku,' the emblems of which form the first subject of illustration, is also a festival of great importance: it takes place about the middle of June, which is the fifth month of the Japanese calendar, from which it derives its designation, and is kept up with more than ordinary spirit during the three days of its continuance. It is held in commemoration

B

of Gongen Sama, the great general to whom the present dynasty owes its existence; and the Japanese date their births from this festival, even if born the day after its last celebration.

It has several curious symbols, the most striking being huge aerial fishes, in imitation of the 'koi,' or 'carp;' large crimson streamers, representations of Gongen Sama crushing a demon; and the heads and tails of crayfish, with which they decorate their dishes and the entrances of their houses. The floating fish flag is hoisted over every house in which a boy has been born during the preceding twelve months, and is emblematical of his future career. As the 'koi,' or 'carp,' which is very plentiful in Japan, finds its way up streams and rivers, surmounting all obstacles in its way, and rendering itself by its fecundity and edible qualities useful to the whole country, so the child is to make his way through life, boldly fulfilling his destiny, and proving himself a useful and beneficial member of the community. In the same way, the scarlet streamer indicates the birth of a female child, and the domestic nature of her duties. The crayfish are used to remind the people of their humble origin (it being traditionary that the empire originated from a race of poor fishermen), and the consequent necessity of humility, temperance, and frugality, in their different stations in life.*

Various qualities are ascribed to the hero of this festival: he is considered the especial champion of women, for whose protection he instituted several laws and regulations; among others, making it obligatory on them to blacken their teeth on entering into the married state. He is believed to be able to charm away fevers, to alleviate suffering, and to prevent the lives of his *protégées* from being embittered by jealousy. During the celebration of this festival the whole country presents an extraordinary appearance; aerial fishes, streamers, and bamboo decorations,

---

* The slice of salt-fish which accompanies Japanese letters is an exhortation to the same effect.

meet the eye in every direction ; and the people in gala costume, which is always worn on holidays, greatly enhance the brilliancy of the scene.

The gala dress is much gayer than that ordinarily worn, but there is little difference in the material, the dress of every class being regulated by stringent sumptuary laws. Blues and purples predominate in winter, the lighter and more varied colours being generally confined to materials only adapted for summer use. The ladies have a great partiality for crimson crape, which is generally worn as an under-robe, and peeps daintily out at the bottom of the dress, and at the wide open sleeves ; it is also entwined in the hair, and with the girdle, at the back of which it is allowed to droop in full, graceful folds. The men do not affect such bright colours as the women and children, although their robes are often fantastically embroidered with various strange devices, such as shell-fish, frogs, flowers, and landscapes, some of which are beautifully worked.

The whole populace on these occasions seem determined to enjoy themselves ; the air of good-natured contentment, which characterises them at all times, taking a more exuberant tone as they stroll about the streets, visit in family parties, or make excursions to the neighbouring tea-houses. Thoroughly domestic

Mother and Child.
[From Photograph.]

in their tastes and habits, it is a pleasing sight to watch the family groups. Here a grand-dame is carefully assisted along by her son and daughter-in-law, preceded by chattering grandchildren in the gayest of dresses, tugging at extraordinary kites ; or a father, in the doorway of his house, nurses one child, while the mother exhibits for the admiration of sympathizing friends another infant — probably one of the unconscious objects of all this rejoicing.

Though the men frequently exceed the bounds of sobriety on these

festivals and holidays, they rarely become quarrelsome. It is, however, by no means unusual for them to keep in a state of intoxication for days; alleging this, with perfect *sang froid,* as an excuse for any neglected promise or unfinished job.

The 'Omatsurie,' or 'Merchants' Great Festival,' which is only celebrated in the principal towns, takes place about the middle of July, and may be considered to be an exhibition of the different trades, as the merchants and craftsmen of the country show the choicest specimens of their wares

Travelling Merchant. [Native Drawing.]

and handicraft in a kind of trades' procession. Like all the rest of their festivals it has a religious signification, the people believing that misfortunes in business are warded off by it. Upwards of five hundred trade trophies figure in one of these processions, the imposing nature of which may be imagined from the gorgeous materials and fantastic dresses depicted in the illustration. The car in the foreground bears the trophy of the wax-figure makers, whose trade is one of the most lucrative in Japan, as the Japanese not only perpetuate their celebrities by wax-work effigies, but the majority of the people, being professors of the Sintoo religion, have Lares and Penates of the same material, called 'Kamis,' which are supposed to intercede on their behalf with the Supreme Being. And this is in addition to regular wax-work exhibitions, which are very popular, and the sale of toys which are hawked about the country by travelling dealers.

The merchants have a general right of *entrée* to all parts of the town on these occasions. In the illustration, the procession is passing through the official quarter of Yeddo, the Tycoon's palace forming the subject of the

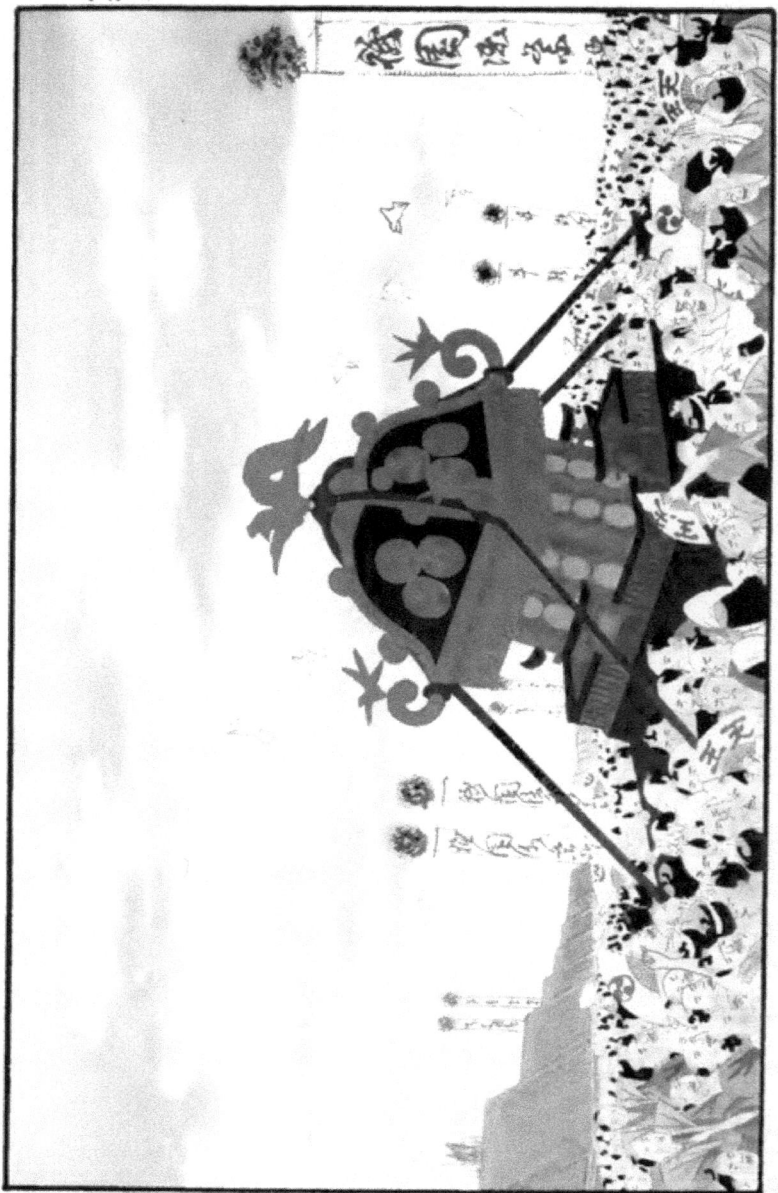

background. They halt from time to time in their progress, which is enlivened by songs descriptive of their various callings, and the beating of huge drums, and blowing of strange discordant instruments. There is a kind of analogy between our industrial exhibitions and these festivals ; and, whatever the purpose may be for which they were originated, it is plain that they admirably represent the industry, wealth, and resources of the country.

'Otinta Sama' is a comical divinity, who is laughed at by some, and believed by others to inhabit certain miniature temples, which are crowned with cocks with outspread wings, as that bird is supposed to be his favourite incarnation. On holidays and festivals, his temples are frequently carried about on the shoulders of his votaries, who are generally the most ignorant and superstitious of the people. This is always a subject of merriment with the unbelievers, who crowd round the temples and oppose their progress,

Saki-drunk.
[Native Drawing.]

and indulge in witticisms at the expense of the divinity and his bearers. This sometimes leads to a disturbance, but only when the parties concerned have been indulging too freely in their favourite saki.

The intercession of Otinta Sama is principally sought in times of drought or of heavy rains ; the temple in the one case being brought out and exposed to the sun, and in the other sprinkled with water, by way of intimating the immediate necessity for his good offices.

CHAPTER II.

FIRES are necessarily frequent, as the majority of the houses are constructed of wood; and such dangerous articles as paper-lanterns, small charcoal fire-boxes, and movable open stoves, for household purposes, are in common use. The candles burnt in the paper-lanterns render them extremely dangerous, as they are fixed by a socket inside the lower end of the candle, which fits on a peg in the lantern—generally very loosely; and as they flare a great deal, very little wind or motion will cause a conflagration. Fires are mostly attributed, however, to the 'chebache,' or small charcoal fire-box, which is used for smoking purposes. It is placed on a small stand in the middle of the thickly-matted rooms, the smokers sitting round drinking saki, and occasionally filling their small pipes. Their method of smoking, like all the rest of their habits, is remarkably peculiar; for, after inhaling a few whiffs, the smoker invariably knocks out the half-consumed remnant on the 'chebache,' and, presently refilling, commences another pipe, and so on, two or three times in succession, rarely troubling himself about the ashes of the last, which the slightest current of air may carry unperceived to smoulder in the combustible flooring.

Fires occur frequently, notwithstanding the great precautions which are taken for their prevention. Town and country are divided into districts, for which certain of the inhabitants are responsible. Each of these has its alarum, with observatory and regular watchers: while every

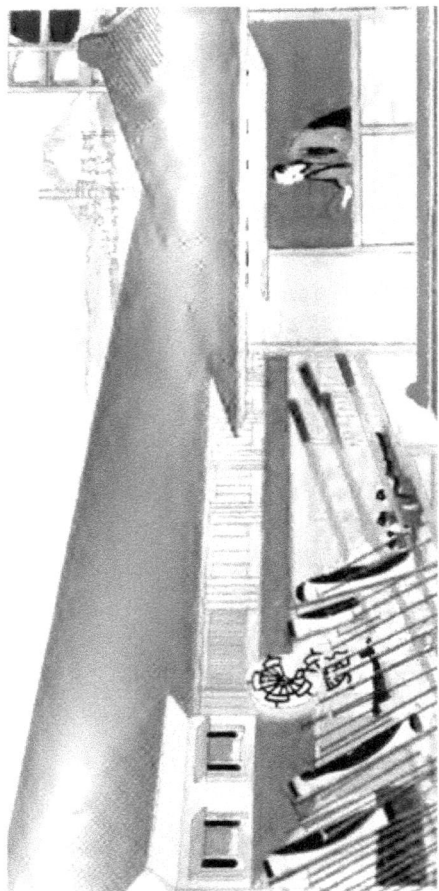

guard-house is provided with a supply of ladders, buckets, and other necessary implements. Whenever a gale is coming on, the 'Yoshongyee and Kanabo,' or 'watch and fire look-outs,' who on ordinary occasions only go their rounds by night, parade the towns with rattles and clanking iron instruments, as a warning to the people to keep their fires low.

They have numerous fire-brigades, which are well organized, and remarkably efficient. In the illustration one of them is seen hurrying along the street to the place of action. On the right, a watchman is striking an alarum, and another may be noticed, half-way up an observatory in the distance, pointing out the direction of the fire. The white building on the other side of the street is a fire-proof storehouse, in which the public documents and valuables of the district are deposited whenever a fire breaks out in it.

A Japanese 'Sheease,' or fire-brigade, passing silently along the streets, lighted by its weird red-and-black distinguishing lanterns, is a strange sight. Some of its members wear armour, with helmets and black-lacquered iron visors, and carry 'martoe,' or 'fire-charms,' and various

Yoshongyee and Kanabo.
[Native Drawing.]

necessary implements; others are clad in head-and-shoulder pieces and gauntlets of light chain-armour, to protect them while pulling down and unroofing houses, which is their especial duty. All have a regular fire costume, from the 'Oki Yaconin,' or 'head man,' to the bare-legged coolie, who carries the badge of the brigade in large red characters on his back. On arriving at a fire, a *point de tête* is selected — generally a house, on the roof of which the fire-charms are immediately fixed, as if to forbid its further advance. These charms (the circular white objects with black mouldings) have, of course, as little effect on one element as Canute's

celebrated command had on another; but the people put such faith in
their virtue that their presence is a powerful auxiliary in prescribing
the limits of fires, which are rarely allowed to pass the bounds marked out
by them. The firemen fight with the flames as they close on the charms,
like men determined to stand by their colours to the last, rushing into the
burning houses, pulling them down, and drenching the blazing thatch, with
great courage and endurance. When, by thus putting their shoulder to the
wheel, the fire is fairly subdued, they turn round and point exultingly to the
martoe as the Hercules that has procured the result. On one occasion, at a
fire in the village of Omura, adjoining Yokahama, the charms and their supporters were actually licked by the flames from the house opposite to that on
which they were fixed, whose thatched roof was pulled off while in a state of
rampant ignition by fire-coolies, who with bare hands, and no other protection than their saturated clothing, fought with the actual fire. One plucky
fellow fell through the roof while thus employed, and, as the spectators still
shuddered at his anticipated fate, rushed out apparently uninjured, and,
re-ascending, resumed his fiery task with unabated vigour. Although the
fire-charms were triumphant on this occasion, they did not escape unscorched,
and several engines had to be kept in constant play upon them and their
supporters, to prevent the one from ignition, and the other from being
baked in their armour like crabs in their shells.

The engines in present use are made of wood, and, though simple,
are efficient in damping the roofs of houses (which, being tiled with thin
squares of wood, are very inflammable), putting out embers, and playing
upon the firemen, who, as already indicated, prefer being stewed to being
roasted. The Japanese, however, are thoroughly aware of the superiority
of our engines, which will probably soon take the place of their own, as
the people are singularly quick in availing themselves of anything useful.

The townspeople generally calculate on being burnt out once in every
seven years, and whenever this calamity falls upon them, no time is lost in
rebuilding. For instance, in December, 1864, a fragment of blazing wood,

from a fire which destroyed the United Service Club at Yokohama, was blown across to the village of Omura before alluded to, which was half burnt down, greatly endangering the General Small-Pox Hospital and the huts of the Royal Marine Battalion in its rear. But early next morning, while the embers of the old houses were still smoking, new ones were in course of erection, and before night some of the industrious occupants were fairly roofed in afresh.*

* As an illustration of the spirit which characterises British merchants in their intercourse with the Japanese, it may be mentioned that a liberal subscription was promptly got up for the re-establishment of these burnt-out villagers ; but, although the Japanese Government seemed thoroughly to appreciate the kindly spirit in which it was offered, national pride came in the way of its acceptance, and the people were only induced to waive their objection on its being urgently pressed upon them that the fire which destroyed the Foreigners' Club was the cause of the calamity.

CHAPTER III.

DOMESTIC LIFE.

It is impossible to mark the even and peaceable tenor of Japanese life, the politeness, industry, respect for superiors, and general air of cheerfulness and content, that pervades all classes, without admiration of the wise regulations which preserve such order amongst them as a people. Quarrels and blows are almost unknown in families ; the husband is gentle, the wife exemplary and affectionate, and the children singularly obedient and reverent to their parents : yet 'Spare the rod and spoil the child ' is a precept totally disregarded. The children are never beaten, nor do the parents allow themselves to lose their tempers in rebuking them, however great the provocation may be—one remarkable result of the complete self-abnegation inculcated by their social system.

The relative position of father and son is very striking. From an early age the latter enjoys the entire confidence of the former, who not only treats him as a grown-up person, but frequently refers disputed matters to his arbitration, invariably abiding by his decision. Again, on a son's arriving at manhood, the parents often resign their property in his favour, relying on him, with a confidence rarely misplaced, for maintenance during the remainder of their lives ; and so sacred is this trust considered, that in case of the son's demise it devolves indisputably on his wife and children. So far, what could be more promising ? But, alas ! like everything else, Japanese life has a dark side, and in this case it consists of a repulsive custom,

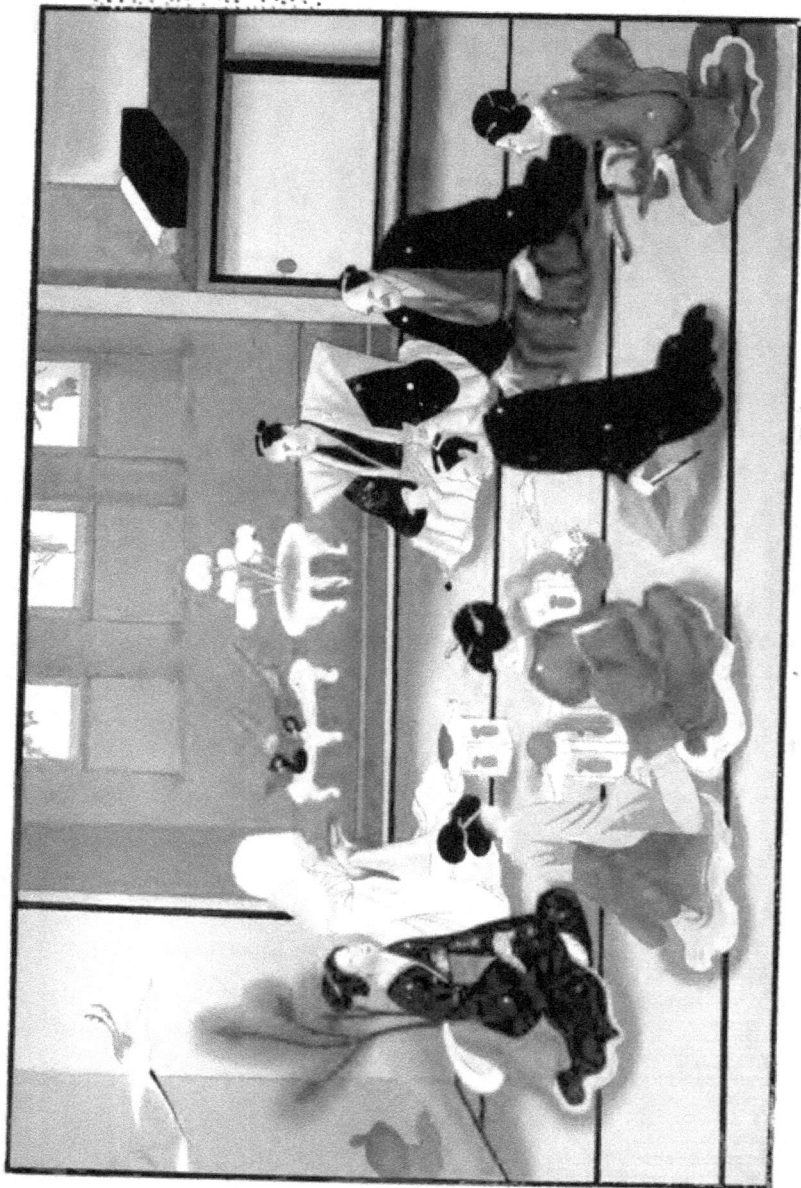

which permits indigent parents to sell their daughters for a term of years into a state of bondage, for purposes of the most degrading nature. This possibility more than counterbalances all the brighter features of their domestic economy. Generally speaking, when young girls find themselves a burden to their parents, they seek employment in the tea-houses, where they are well looked after and instructed in various accomplishments, for which they serve a certain apprenticeship, and at its expiration generally marry, as girls so educated are eagerly sought after.

There are two forms of marriage, either of which is legally binding. One is a religious, and the other a civil contract, not very dissimilar from our marriage by the registrar, saving that the bride's parents sign for her. Whichever form is used, the parents receive a sum of money from the bridegroom ; but in neither case is the husband supposed to see the face of his bride until all due formalities have been performed. The religious ceremony takes place in a temple : the pair, after listening to a lengthy harangue from one of the attendant priests, approach the altar, where large tapers are presented to them ; the bride, instructed by the priest, lights her taper at the sacred censer on the altar, and the bridegroom, igniting his from hers, allows the two flames to combine, and burn steadily together, thus symbolizing the perfect unity of the marriage state ; and this completes the ceremonial.

The illustration represents the private ratification of the civil contract, which is a simple form, by which the parties take upon themselves the respective duties of husband and wife. The veiled figure in white is the 'hanna-yomie,' or 'bride,' in the act of acknowledging the 'hanna-moko,' or 'bridegroom' (who sits opposite to her in an official dress), by partaking of the nuptial saki. This 'saki,' or 'wine,' is prepared by two intimate female friends of the bride, who first pour it into the gold and silver lacquer vessels on the stand, which respectively represent the husband and wife, and then, taking the vessels in hand, mix the contents in a cup, and deliver it to the 'shewarin,' or 'master of the ceremonies,' who hands it to the bride, and then to the bridegroom, and both partake of the contents, which act constitutes the marriage.

Although young ladies are employed to mix the nuptial saki they do not

A Dose of Moxa. [Native Drawing.]

attend on the bride. Such offices as are required are performed by a married couple, the shewarin and his wife. It is they who make the necessary arrangements, and provide the pheasants that appear in the recess; which signify that the hanna-moko, like the cock-pheasant, will always jealously guard his charmer, who, like the shy hen-bird, will readily respond to the call of her mate.

A more practical idea of the requirements of married life may be deduced from the annexed woodcut, representing the application of moxa, which is very commonly used as a remedy for rheumatism, and to promote circulation.

Japanese women make excellent wives: they are never idle in their houses; and when other occupations fail them, the spinning-wheel, or loom, is brought out, and materials for clothing their families are prepared. In the country, the women share equally with their husbands and children in agricultural labours; early and late whole families may be seen in the paddy-fields transplanting rice, or superintending its irrigation, for which the undulating nature of the country affords great facility.

Transplanting Rice. [Native Drawing.]

Notwithstanding the laborious nature of their tasks they have always a cheerful greeting for the passer-by, even under extremely irritating circumstances, as they are greatly plagued by leeches, which swarm in the paddy-fields.

The result of the constant attention paid to the cultivation of the soil is astonishing. Our farmers would gaze with surprise on the luxuriant crops of cereals, roots, and vegetables ; and this is solely owing to the care taken in preparing the soil, which is not naturally productive. Weeds are never to be met with in the fields, which, however, from the constant manuring bestowed upon them, lack the sweet fresh smell of our own.

With regard to education, it is rare to meet with a Japanese who cannot read, write, and cipher ; and in buying and selling they use computing slides like the Chinese, by the aid of which they quickly settle the amount to be paid.   They do not, except in the higher classes, receive what we understand by a general or scientific education, the members of each trade or profession being only instructed in what pertains to their own affairs—a fact the inquiring stranger soon discovers.

CHAPTER IV.

THE TYCOON, DAIMIOS, AND ARISTOCRACY.

THE Government of Japan consists of an oligarchy of feudal princes, called Daimios, wielding absolute authority in their respective provinces, but subject to the general control of one of their number, (selected from one of three great families), called the 'Tycoon,' who, assisted by a 'Gorogio,' or 'Great Council,' presides over the affairs of the state in the name of the 'Mikado,' or 'Spiritual Emperor,' its supreme head.

The office of Mikado is apparently the cause of most of the disturbances which agitate the country. Its temporal importance lies in possessing the power of issuing decrees, bestowing titles, and delegating authority to others; and princes discontented with the Tycoon are constantly intriguing against his legitimate influence with the Mikado. For instance: an attempt was made in 1864 by a powerful coalition, headed by Choisiu, prince of Nangato, to obtain possession of the Mikado's person. This was only prevented after a severe struggle by the bravery of the Tycoon's guard, to whose care the palace and its inmates were entrusted. During the conflict a large portion of the sacred city of Miako was burnt.

The Tycoon only leaves Yeddo when affairs of state require his presence elsewhere. His palace is situated in the heart of the city, and is surrounded by grounds several miles in circumference, and enclosed by a deep moat. It is there that he receives the compulsory visits of the grandees of the empire, one of whom, on the point of being ushered into the audience-chamber, is

shown opposite, in his robes of ceremony, and attended by a sword-bearer, in token of his high rank. The bonze, or priest, who precedes him, does not impart any religious signification to the visit, as priests commonly act in the double capacity of spy and master of the ceremonies. The screen which forms the background of the illustration is worthy of attention, as its subject is taken from the Japanese mythology, and represents the great sun-god from whom Ten-zio-dai-zin, the patron goddess of the empire, sprang.

In public, these oligarchical princes are invariably surrounded by all the pomp of feudal state, and when they travel are escorted by large bodies of retainers. At Kanagawa, which adjoins the settlement of Yokohama, the foreigner has frequent opportunities of witnessing their processions as they pass to and fro along the 'tokaido,' or 'great public road,' when they are going on their compulsory visits to Yeddo from their own country palaces. Nor is much danger attached to this, as the passing of Daimios whom it would be dangerous to meet on the tokaido, is always notified by the authorities to the consul. On witnessing a Daimio's procession for the first time, it is hard to realise that it is not a scene from some gorgeous panto-mime, so brilliant and varied are the costumes of the retainers, and so totally different is it from anything which European eyes are accustomed to gaze upon. But should anything excite the risible faculties of the observer, his hallucinations are likely to be quickly scattered by the scowls of the resolute-looking fellows passing by with 'hand on sword,' needing but little encouragement to 'set a glory' to it, 'by giving it the worship of revenge,' as they are extremely jealous of the honour of their prince, and regard the pre-sence of foreigners on the tokaido at such times as an insult. This circum-stance is also rendered more galling by foreigners sitting coolly on their horses by the road-side as the great man passes, generally in a low norimon, on which they must necessarily look down—in contradiction to Japanese etiquette, which permits no inferior to look down upon a superior—while the people of the country are either abjectly kowtowing to him or patiently waiting in their closed houses until his passing shall set them once more at liberty.

A review given the by two ministers for foreign affairs to Sir Rutherford
Alcock, shortly before his departure, was a very imposing spectacle.   The
approach of the ministers was announced by the beating of drums (which are
sometimes carried on the shoulder and struck by the palm of the hand) and
the blowing of conch-shells, each instrument being sounded three times in
succession, at short intervals.   Men in armour carrying banners, bearing the
Tycoon's crest, headed the procession.   They were followed by a large drum
in a square case, carried by two men, and the conch-blowers ; then came a
number of spearmen in armour ; officers on horseback immediately preceding
the ministers.   On arriving at the ground they dismounted, and were received
by Sir Rutherford Alcock, the remainder of their retinue passing on and
forming in rear of the others, to the left of the English garrison, consisting
of the second battalion of the 20th Regiment, the Royal Marine battalion, and
detachments of Royal Artillery, of the 67th Regiment, and Beloochees, who
were drawn up in brigade in honour of the occasion.   At the request of the
ministers the garrison marched past and performed a few manœuvres, con-
cluding with discharging blank cartridge in squares and in skirmishing order.
The rapidity of the fire appeared to make a great impression on them.   This
over, the Japanese performance commenced ; which was a representation of
their ancient order of battle, the retainers dividing and forming in lines opposite one another, and about one hundred yards apart.   The proceedings were
conducted by two marshals on foot ; they began by forming the spearmen in
line, with emphatic guttural commands, stamping of the feet, and flourishing
of gilt bâtons, to the end of which wisps of paper were attached.   All were
habited in magnificent armour : some wore complete suits of mail ; others
chain armour, lined with gorgeous silks.   Broad lacquered hats were here
and there substituted for helmets ; or both were dispensed with, and the
temples of the combatants bound with linen cloth, which is their usual head-
dress in action.   Presently a signal was given, on which the opposing lines
commenced simultaneously to ' mark line double.'   At a second signal they
faced into Indian file, and the marshals, placing themselves at their head,

led them off at a swinging trot, the whole party flinging up their heels like boys playing at 'follow my leader,' until startling guttural shouts from the marshals caused the glittering lines to halt and face each other. The horsemen, who had hitherto taken no part in the pageant, were now stationed in rear of the centre of the respective lines, and added greatly to the effect by their crested helmets, their richly gilt armour, and the heraldic banners, which were attached to the back of the cuirass and floated about two feet over their heads. As soon as the horsemen were stationed the exciting part of the sham-fight began, by the lines being wheeled backwards and forwards in wings from the centre, and into zigzag formations from central points, with a slow 'stamp-and-go' march, the spears being flourished with each motion and pointed high and low, and right and left, as in our bayonet exercise. The marshals regulated the movements of their respective lines with great accuracy, the one being retired directly the other advanced, so that the relative distance was never altered. After a time both parties suddenly assumed a sitting posture

A Daimios Retainer.   (Native Drawing.)

and exchanged howls of defiance, which grew fiercer and fiercer, until a simultaneous rush, as if to engage, finished the performance, from which the representatives of barbaric warfare retired amid the hearty cheers of the representatives of the bayonet and rifle.

Though most of the Daimios have enormous revenues, and are surrounded by men devotedly attached to them, the policy of the country so trammels their actions with formalities and espionage as to keep them in considerable subjection to the Tycoon ; nor is even the privacy of their houses respected.

for their families are retained in Yeddo, as hostages for their good behaviour, while they are absent in their principalities. As an occasional relaxation from the cares attendant on their high position, they avail themselves of a privilege called 'naiboen,' which enables them to share incognito in the pleasures and amusements of their countrymen. Those drawings and coloured representations of scenes connected with the higher classes which so largely engross the attention of Japanese artists, generally depict naiboen intrigues and adventures: these convey, however, a very exaggerated idea of the manner in which the Daimios conduct themselves on these occasions.

The family in the house-boat witnessing a pyrotechnic display in the bay of Yeddo, may be regarded as a faithful representation of a Daimio's party enjoying the naiboen. The great man in his light summer robe has apparently cast aside the cares of office, and seems thoroughly to enjoy the cool evening breeze and the society of his wives, only one of whom has a legal claim to that title, by right of which she takes precedence of the others. Of the two bonzes, or priests, in the stern of the boat, one, probably, is a member of the family, and the other its spy, for even naiboen excursions are not exempted from espionage: indeed the Japanese are so habituated to this custom that they generally regard it as a necessary check upon themselves. Naiboen excursions to the tea-houses are very frequent, notice being sent previously in order to insure proper accommodation and privacy; the latter precaution being principally taken on account of the ladies of the family, who never go beyond the palace except in a norimon guarded by armed retainers.

Coolies carrying Norimon.
[From Native Drawing.]

In their homes, the aristocracy are as simple in their habits as the rest of

the people. They are much given to study, the favourite subjects being poetry,* history, astronomy, and logic. The children are usually taught the rudiments of education by their mothers, and as they advance in years, are either privately instructed by masters or sent to the great schools at Miako, which are said to be attended by upwards of four thousand scholars.

* A very interesting volume of translations of Japanese Lyrical Odes has lately been published by F. V. Dickins, Esq. M.B. Smith, Elder, & Co.

CHAPTER V.

THE COURT OF THE MIKADO.

THE spiritual Emperor of Japan is supposed to be a direct descendant of the gods, and as such enjoys the adoration, as well as the fealty of his subjects. Unfortunately, his divine attributes deprive him of the free exercise of his human functions, as his feet are never permitted to touch the ground out of doors; nor is he allowed to cut his hair, beard, or nails, or to expose himself to the rays of the sun, which would detract from the excellency of his person. His principal titles are, 'Zen Zi,'—'Son of Heaven;' 'Mikado,'—'Emperor;' and 'Dairi,' or 'Kinrai,'—'Grand Interior:' the latter denoting the perpetual seclusion of his person. It is said that his ancestry can be traced in an unbroken line from nearly 700 years before the Christian era.

The Mikado never goes beyond the precincts of the Imperial residence, which occupies a large portion of the city of Miako, comprising numerous palaces and gardens; and connected with it are the schools alluded to in the last chapter, which are established on the plan of a university, and are much resorted to by the children of the nobility.

Whenever this great personage wishes to take an airing, he is carried by fourteen men in a large norimon with latticed windows, through which he is able to see without being seen; and even when granting an audience he is said to be concealed from view by bamboo screen-work. His court consists of the members of his own family and certain great officers of state appointed

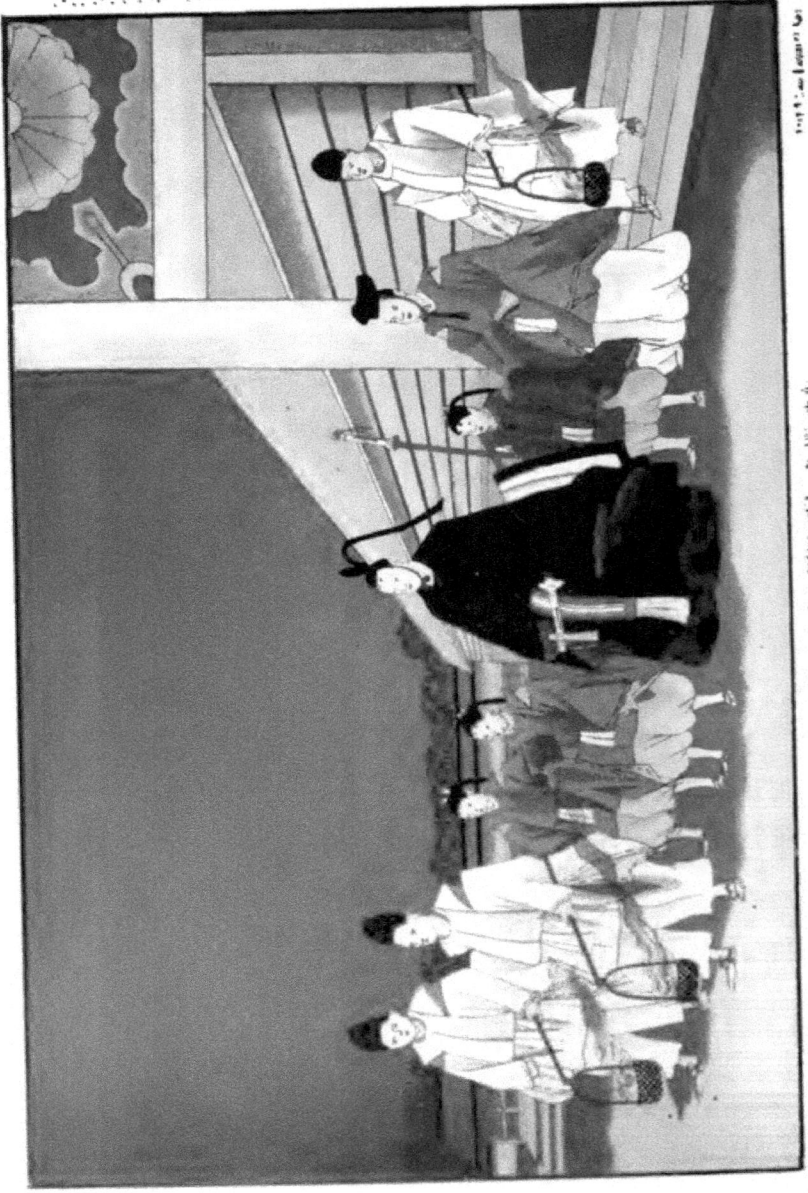

by the Tycoon, who nominally receive and promulgate his commands; but, in ordinary times, he has no real power in the temporal affairs of the empire, and only refuses to confer legality on the acts of his lieutenant under the pressure of intrigue, or of undue family influence.

To relieve the wearisome monotony of his life, as well as to prevent the possibility of the sacred race becoming extinct, he is allowed twelve wives, who are chosen from the most beautiful daughters of the chief princes of the empire. These ladies occupy separate palaces in the immediate vicinity of his, where they are attended by their own retainers; but only one of them enjoys the rank of empress, although they are all treated with the deference due to royalty. He is also said to have an unlimited number of concubines, who reside within the bounds of the Imperial establishment.

The distinctive mark of the members of the Mikado's court and of the ladies of his family consists of two black patches placed on the forehead, and in the arrangement of the hair, which is gathered up in a long cue and curved over the head by one sex, and worn dishevelled and without any kind of ornament by the other. Though the Mikado has little influence in the secular affairs of state, his authority in religious questions is supreme: but it is doubtful if he personally takes any part in the solemnities which are constantly occurring at Miako.

The subject of illustration represents one of these sacred observances: the procession is coming from the Mikado's palace, which, properly speaking, is a temple, being full of idols and effigies of the 'Kamis,' or 'canonised saints.' The principal figure is the third minister of state, and from this circumstance the white dresses worn by the 'Kargardhee,' or 'fire-bearers,' and the presence of some of the Imperial children, it is probably a midnight pilgrimage to some neighbouring shrine, in honour of the manes of a departed member of the family.

The early education of the Mikado's children is entrusted to the ladies of the court: the sons, while still young, are sent to different religious fraternities; and the daughters, on attaining a suitable age, are bestowed in

marriage on the nobles of the country, except the eldest, who is appointed
chief priestess of the temple of the Sun at Issie, which contains the shrine of
Ten-zio-dai-zin, to which all Japanese are supposed to make a pilgrimage
once in their lifetime.

The Mikado is said to spend the greatest portion of his time in the
society of his wives, who contribute to his amusement by singing, dancing,
and theatrical entertainments.   The latter sometimes take place in the
open air, as in the scene depicted opposite ; on which the 'Grand Interior'
and a select party are supposed to be
looking down through the jalousies of
the palace. The vocal, instrumental,
and theatrical talents of the performers, are here called into play, the
arena for the latter being the 'Me-
koshee,' or movable stage, in which
a female figure may be noticed de-
claiming her part. The long-handled,
fantastically-coloured umbrellas, belong
to the Imperial attendants taking part
in the theatricals, whose hair, it will
be noticed, is arranged according to
court etiquette.

The men whose features are concealed by their broad hats are 'Nin-

A Begging Criminal. [Native Drawing.]

sokee,' or 'public singers.' Generally speaking they belong to the aristocratic
class, and are reduced to earn their livelihood in this manner in consequence
of some misdemeanour, on account of which their property has been forfeited
to the state. Their occupation is in itself a punishment, as Japanese gentlemen
never sing, regarding that accomplishment as derogatory to their dignity.
A certain class of criminals also wear a disguise of this nature, as shown in
the woodcut.

The band here represented is much stronger than those that generally figure in Japanese orchestral and theatrical entertainments. Music is not used, as with us, to fill the interval between the pieces, but accompanies the performers throughout; the louder instruments being energetically struck as the singing becomes impassioned or the actors declamatory.

The butterfly dance is another specimen of the amusements with which the ladies of the Mikado's court while away their monotonous existence. As here shown, it is a private performance, of which the Empress and her principal attendants are the only spectators. The insects are personated by two of her ladies, who mimic their motions and sing praises of the different flowers they pretend to alight upon, to the accompaniment of a band of fair musicians. But the most interesting part of the affair is a spirited dialogue, in which they cleverly criticise, under floral appellations, the different ladies of the court, in a manner equally gratifying and flattering to their royal mistress.

Lady waiting on the Mikado. [From Photograph.]

The Mikado is always waited upon by the ladies of his court, and is said never to eat twice from the same vessels, which are broken to pieces as soon as they are removed. An intelligent yaconin, however, on being questioned about this point, was much amused; and, though he professed ignorance of the subject, was evidently very sceptical on the matter of the dishes.

CHAPTER VI.

THE 'HARA KIRU.'

ALTHOUGH we have long been aware of the existence of this peculiar mode of suicide, the exclusive policy of the Japanese has placed insuperable difficulties in the way of obtaining accurate information concerning it.

A more enlightened policy is now gaining ground in the country. The chromo-lithographs that illustrate these 'Sketches' are fac-similes of paintings by native artists, selected from a series lately published at Yeddo, and sold to foreigners with the connivance, if not by permission, of the authorities; for the spy system in Japan is so perfect, that illicit dealings are next to impossible.

As Japanese punishments entail disgrace on every member of the culprit's family, the 'Hara Kiru,' or 'happy dispatch,' which is the only exception, is regarded as a great privilege by the classes entitled to avail themselves of it. These consist of the nobility, military, and officials of a certain rank holding civil appointments.

It seems to be a prevalent idea that this sacrifice is reserved for political offences; but this is not the case, as crimes of all descriptions are condoned by it.

A simple act of suicide does not constitute the 'Hara Kiru.' To render the act legal, and to ensure the heir and family of the person performing it against disgrace and loss of property, an order for its performance must be issued by the Tycoon, or by the suzerain prince of the culprit.

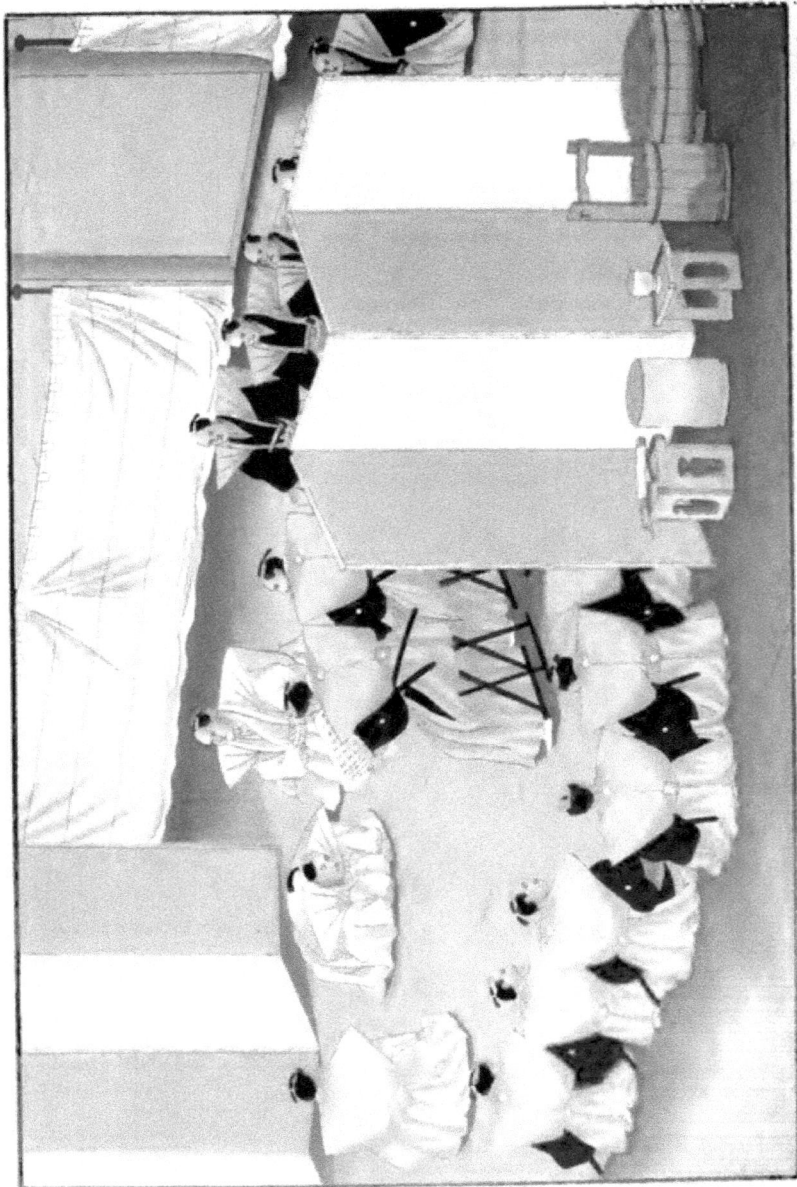

The Japanese, being a high-spirited and patriotic people, consider that death under any circumstances is preferable to dishonour; and the privileged classes always carry about with them when they travel the paraphernalia used at the performance of the 'Hara Kiru,' in token of their readiness to prove their patriotism, or to die rather than disgrace their family.

The dress consists of a robe and 'harakama,' or 'winged official dress,' of coarse white cloth—white being the funeral colour of the country—which is undistinguished by the crest or any sign of the rank of the owner. There is also the disembowelling knife, the blade of which is about eight inches long, and very sharp.

When the sentence of the 'Hara Kiru' is awarded, or the humble request of a defeated politician to perform it is acceded to, a formal document is made out and duly signed by the competent authorities. It is then delivered to two commissioners, by whom it is conveyed to the culprit.

Should the proposed victim be a Daimio of importance, and sufficiently powerful to set the Tycoon at defiance, the delivery of the imperial mandate is likely to be attended with unpleasant results, as the bearers are sometimes waylaid and murdered by retainers of the doomed prince, and have frequently to resort to stratagem to accomplish their task. But when once the mandate is delivered, the prince must submit, or he would lose caste even with his own followers, so strongly are the Japanese imbued with respect for the ancient customs of their country.

The accompanying illustrations represent the different formalities that are observed at the performance of the 'Hara Kiru' by a Daimio.

On receiving the official intimation of his sentence, he orders the necessary preparations to be made, and informs his friends and relatives of it, inviting them to share in a parting carouse with him.

On the appointed day, after taking a private farewell of his family, he receives his friends. He is habited in his white robes, and supported by two of his relatives or ministers, similarly attired. When the time arrives (which is previously arranged with the commissioners) he takes leave of the guests,

E

as on any ordinary occasion, and enters the screened enclosure, accompanied
by his supporters. It will be noticed, that the retainers guarding the
exterior and entrance are barefooted, which is a mark of respect in honour of
the rank of the culprit, and of the solemnity of the occasion.

The Tycoon's messengers then read the imperial mandate, which proclaims that, in accordance with the ancient custom of the country, the
Daimio is permitted honourably to sacrifice himself for its benefit, and
thus to expiate in his own person the crime or offence he has committed
against the welfare of the state. In the illustration, the two officials
charged with this disagreeable office are sitting opposite the Daimio and
his friends, reading the fatal document, their suite surrounding them in
respectful attitudes.

The whole party wear the official dress, which intimates at once the
respect due to the victim and the official nature of the ceremony.

The second scene shows the Daimio on the point of performing the
sacrificial ceremony. His forelock is reversed, as a sign of submission
to his fate, and to assist the executioner, who, as soon as his master goes
through the form of disembowelling himself with the knife on the stand,
will, with one blow of his razor-edged sword, complete the sacrifice by
decapitation. Only the two chief commissioners appointed by the Tycoon,
and the sorely-tasked supporters of the victim, remain to witness the last
act of the drama. The rest of the party await its completion in the adjoining compartment of the enclosure, which is expressly constructed for that
purpose.

The funeral procession, which is the subject of the next scene, is accompanied by all the pomp indicative of the high position of the deceased.
The mourners wear robes of white cloth, and all the feudal paraphernalia are
draped with the same material; which, as before mentioned, is used in
Japanese mourning. The coffin is carried near the head of the procession:
it is a square box of resinous wood, covered over with white, and the
body is placed in it in a sitting posture.

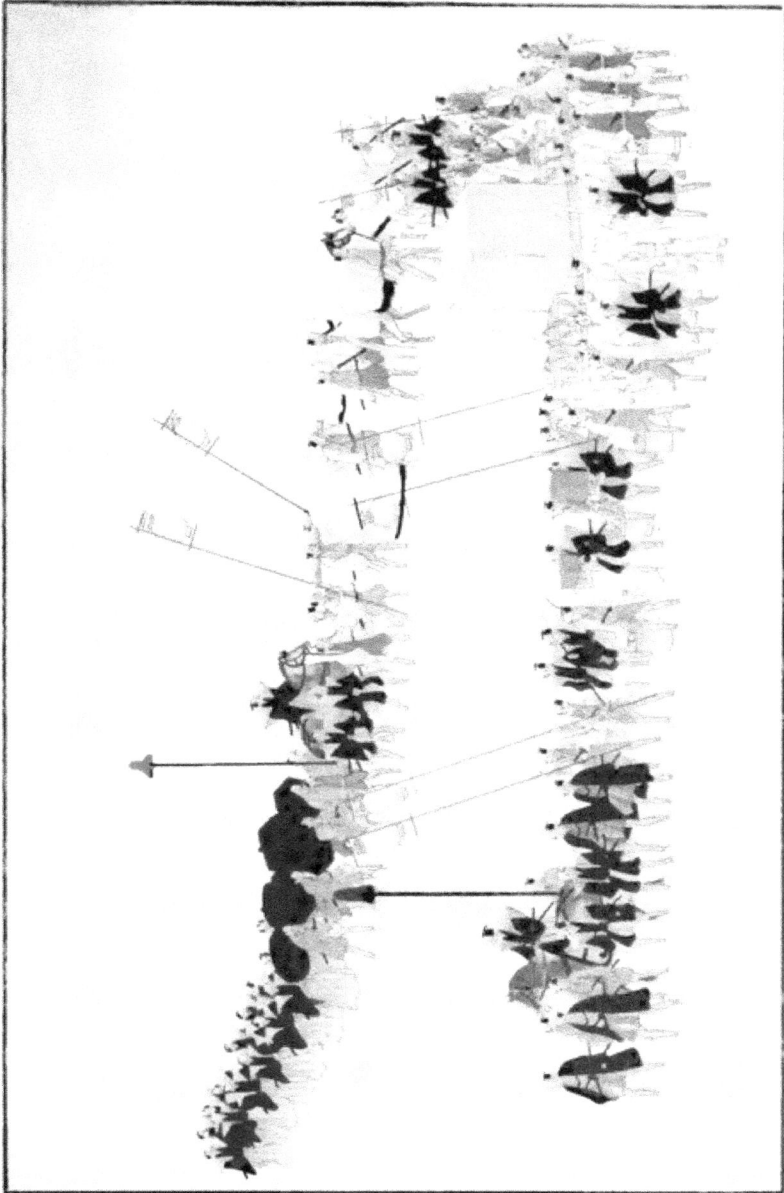

All the members of the family attend the funeral, either on foot or in norimons. If the wife and the heir be absent in Yeddo, they are represented by the nearest relations. In this instance both are present, from which it may be inferred that the sacrificial act has taken place in the neighbourhood of Yeddo.

Although the Japanese sometimes bury their dead, they generally practise cremation. Repulsive as this custom is to European ideas, it must be remembered that the Japanese are not singular in preferring it, as several of the most civilised nations of antiquity considered it the most honourable mode of disposing of the bodies of the dead. While the body is being reduced to ashes the priests tell their beads and chant prayers for the soul of the departed, as the followers of almost every religious sect in Japan believe in a state of purgatory.

The last scene shows the wife and son of the victim of the 'Hara Kiru' collecting his ashes and depositing them in an earthenware jar. This is afterwards sealed down and conveyed to the cemetery, or temple, which contains the remains of his ancestors.

Some of the Japanese cemeteries are very extensive; and they are generally situated in secluded, picturesque spots, in the neighbourhood of the towns and villages.

The graves are small, round, cemented receptacles, just large enough to receive the jar containing the ashes. If the body is buried (which only happens when the deceased is friendless, or too poor to pay the expenses of cremation), the head is always placed pointing to the north. The tombstones are ordinarily about three feet high; and are either square or circular in shape, resting on square pedestals, in which small holes are cut to contain rice and water. The supplies of these are replenished from time to time, generally by the women of the family, lest the spirit of the deceased should revisit its grave and imagine itself neglected. Sometimes flowers are placed before the graves, and flowering sprigs of peach and plum are stuck in the ground about them.

Like the Chinese, the Japanese burn joss-sticks to propitiate the deities in favour of their departed relatives; and the neighbourhood of a grave-yard may generally be detected by the peculiar aromatic odour emitted during the burning of these. For some time after a funeral the relatives daily visit the tomb and intercede for the dead, holding their hands up in the attitude of prayer, and rubbing the palms together as they mutter their monotonous orisons.

CHAPTER VII.

NATIONAL GAMES AND AMUSEMENTS.

NOTWITHSTANDING the industrious habits of the Japanese, they are great lovers of pleasure, and much addicted to sight-seeing; theatres and wax-work exhibitions are very numerous, and jugglers, top-spinners, and tumblers, are regular *habitués* of the streets.

Though they do not allow pleasure to come before business, they do not hesitate to associate it with religious observances; and on solemn festival occasions, the vicinity of even the most sacred temples is occupied by a variety of shows and common stalls, for the sale of sweetmeats, toys, and coloured pictures.

Their principal athletic amusement is wrestling, which may be regarded as the national game of the country. It is very generally practised, and pairs of 'brawny fellows' are to be frequently met with of an evening in the outskirts of towns and villages, either crouched down in the preliminary attitude, which resembles that of angry fighting-cocks, or dragging one another to and fro like frogs struggling over a choice morsel. The game is necessarily a dragging and pulling one, its grand object being to force the opponent beyond a certain boundary.

So popular is it, that in addition to public performers, who travel about the country exhibiting their prowess, the Daimios keep private bands: each district has some especial champion; and every Japanese a favourite '*smoo*,' as they term the wrestlers, whose exploits are canvassed with an enthusiasm totally at variance with the stolid indifference which usually characterises the people, when any subject is broached that does not directly concern their ordinary vocations.

The professional wrestlers are generally men of herculean proportions. From constant practice they attain a muscular development that would eclipse that of our prize-ring champions ; but their paunchy figures and sluggish movements render any further comparison impossible, as they neither practise nor appreciate what we call training. Size and weight are prized more than activity in the limited arena to which their performances are confined : so, instead of walking down superabundant flesh, they endeavour to increase it, dieting themselves on rice and fish, which is far from productive of any Bantingite result. The illustration of the Great Wrestling Amphitheatre at Yeddo conveys a fair idea of the estimation in which athletic games are held by the Japanese. The enclosure is capable of containing several thousand spectators, and is always filled when a match of importance takes place.

In the centre is the '*docho*,' or 'boundary-ring,' which is about eighteen feet in diameter. The game is generally decided by one or other of the combatants being forced against this boundary ; for, although a fair throw counts, it rarely decides the mastery, as the great weight and the crouching position of the wrestlers necessitate dragging, pushing, and even carrying ; and the tenacity of their grasp is such, that any other results are almost impossible.

The price of admission to these exhibitions is very low ; and, like everything else of a public nature, is regulated by the government. Officials are appointed to superintend the arrangements, and to see that no accidents arise from overcrowding. For this purpose they are provided with a box that overlooks the whole building.

The lofty scaffolding outside the enclosure is a time stage, from which the commencement and duration of each match are intimated to the audience by a certain number of strokes on the drum that surmounts it.

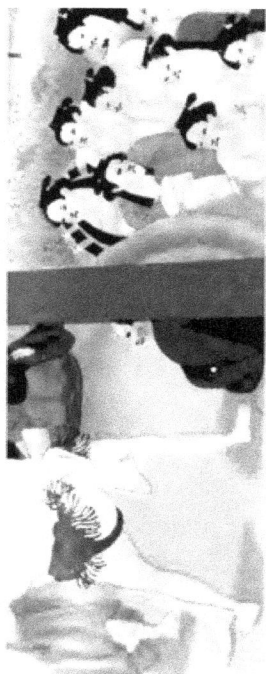

Before each wrestling-match commences, the 'geogee,' or 'judge,' who superintends it, shouts out the names and exploits of the contenders, who, after kowtowing very ceremoniously to one another, rise to the preliminary attitude.

At a signal from the judge the combatants commence. At first they move cautiously about the centre of the ring, watching a favourable opportunity to close, which they presently do with deep guttural exclamations. Then great working of muscle and tugging and straining follow, the spectators cheering on their respective favourites, until the fall of the geogee's fan—which is the moment depicted by the artist—proclaims the victor.

Thundering plaudits greet the hero of the occasion, who presently strolls about among the assembled multitude, attended by his 'cosgi,' or 'servant,' who collects the offerings with which they liberally reward his exertions. When money fails, articles of clothing are frequently bestowed— and sometimes too freely, as it is by no means unusual for both sexes to half denude themselves at these exhibitions ; and it is a favourite joke with the women to send their male friends to redeem the articles from the wrestler.

Yaconins fencing.

Although fencing is a military exercise, it is so commonly practised by the Japanese 'yaconinierie,' or 'soldiery,' who comprise a large portion of the population, and is entered into by them in so spirited a manner. that it deserves to be classed as an amusement.

The woodcut is a very faithful representation of yaconins fencing. The masks cover the whole of the head ; and the arms, breast, and hips. are protected by cuirass, petticoat, &c. of leather ribbed with bamboo.

The fencing-sticks are of the same length as the 'obi-todee-auf-catana.'

or 'great fighting-sword.' They are made of split canes, bound tightly together, and are used with both hands.

The Japanese fence well, and deliver their points with great precision, especially an awkward downward thrust at the breast.

They deliver their cuts and points with fierce guttural exclamations, which are peculiarly disagreeable to European ears; especially when the listener is located in the vicinity of a guard-house, whose occupants notify their employment at daybreak with such cries as ' Hie-e! Ah-h! Atturah-h!' (' That's at! that's into you!') and continue this information, accompanied by the clashing of their sticks, and occasional chuckles, until late in the afternoon.

The Japanese are great frequenters of the theatres, of the interior of one of which the illustration is a very good representation—the exterior is generally very like that of the temples; and in some, the ground-floor is laid out with miniature lakes and bridges, the audience looking down on the performance from lateral and opposite galleries.

The stage is a little smaller than ours, but sometimes has a promenade through the centre of the theatre, which facilitates by-play, to which the Japanese attach great importance. The body of the house is divided into boxes, which are generally taken by family parties, who bring their provisions with them and remain all day, as the performances begin about 10 A.M. and last until late in the evening. Their plays are very tedious, although enlivened by a good deal of smart *repartée* and telling jokes, but the morality even of the most correct is very questionable. Love, of course, is the prevailing feature; and the adventures of the principal heroes contain enough bloodshed and murder to satisfy the most ardent admirer of sensation dramas. In their hand-to-hand encounters they cut and slash at one another with naked swords, which they manage very skilfully, never permitting the blades to come into contact. The female parts are performed by boys and young men, who, with the assistance of paint and powder, make admirable sub-

stitutes for women, though singing and dancing-girls are frequently intro-
duced as divertissements.

Getting ready to go to the Theatre.

Kite-flying is also a favourite amusement; and old age and childhood
may frequently be seen side-by-side, tugging at soaring monsters, in the
construction of which great ingenuity is displayed.

The Japanese often play with cards, which are about a quarter of
the size of ours; and they are much given to gambling, although it is
strictly prohibited, and, when detected, severely punished. But the most
popular in-door game is a sort of combination of draughts and chess,
which frequently engrosses the players for hours at a time.

F

CHAPTER VIII.

CRIMES against property are rare in Japan, which is owing to the high-spirited and honourable feelings that actuate all classes of the community; but from the feudal nature of the government, the small value attached to life, and the deadly weapons constantly carried by the military classes, who are notoriously proud and revengeful, crimes against the person are very frequent.

A great check upon criminal offences is the severity of the punishments inflicted, and the disgrace entailed upon the culprit's family.

Although the laws are extremely severe, and in their administration there is neither jury nor counsel, justice is delivered with great impartiality; and the judge, who is generally the governor of the town or district in which the offence has been committed, is entrusted with considerable discretionary power.

When a prisoner is being examined his arms are bound to his sides by a rope, which also passes round his neck, the end of which is held by an official, who, if his charge prove unruly, manages him by pulls and jerks.

'Thrashemono,' or 'public exposure,' is associated with all Japanese punishments, and is said to be in itself a great preventive of crime, as the spirited Japanese dread being held up to the reprobation of their acquaintance more than they fear the extreme penalty of the law.

The illustration, showing the mode of conducting a criminal to execution,

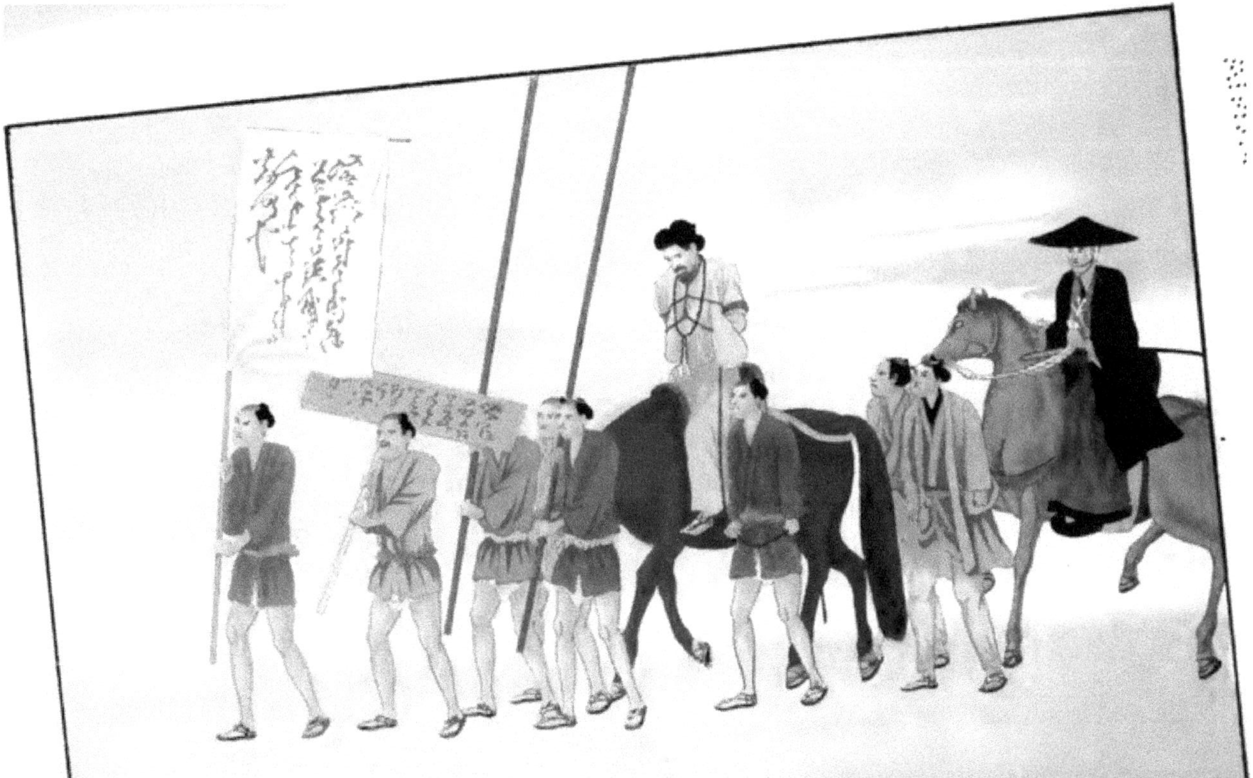

is an instance of 'thrashemono.' The culprit is bound on a horse, and is preceded by a placard, borne by his relatives or neighbours, and indicating his crime. In this manner he is conducted through the town to the place of execution, where his sentence is read to him. He is then placed (with his limbs still bound) over a freshly-dug hole, where he is supported by his relatives till the executioner's sword performs its task.

After execution, the heads of malefactors are generally exposed : that of Simono Sedgi (the lonin who was decapitated in the presence of the British garrison of Yokohama, for being the organizer of the assassination of Major Baldwin and Lieutenant Bird of Her Majesty's 20th Regiment) was exhibited on the public stand at the guard-house at the entrance of the town.

This man was a fair specimen of the lonin type, and was a most determined ruffian, whose whole life had been a career of crime.

When exposed in the streets of Yokohama the day preceding his execution, he conducted himself with great bravado, remarking on the improvements in the town since he last visited it, and expressing his regret that he had not killed a consul.

At the place of execution he made an impassioned speech, in which he declared that he was a gentleman by birth, and had studied the arts and sciences, and never believed the government would sacrifice a Japanese for the death of a foreigner. He said that the days would come when they would repent the encouragement they were now giving to strangers ; and ended by complimenting the executioner on his well-known skill.

The lonin differs from the ordinary criminal, and is thus ably described by the highest authority on Japanese matters : [a]—

' As a noble or head of a house is responsible for all who are of his family, or claim his protection, when any of his people are resolved upon a desperate enterprise they formally renounce the protection and declare themselves "lonins ;"—in other words, outlaws, or friendless men : after

* Sir Rutherford Alcock. See ' Capital of the Tycoon.'

which no one is responsible for their acts, and this is considered a highly honourable and proper thing to do.'

The worst of this system is, that any one harbouring or assisting a lonin endangers his head; and such men are, therefore, compelled to resort to robbery and extortion as means of supporting themselves. It generally happens that this legalised method of taking the law into their own hands drives those who avail themselves of it into a series of crimes, and frequently they become the associates of common thieves.

Of the gang represented in the illustration as robbing a rich merchant's house, one or two probably are lonins, the rest being thieves in disguise.

The servants, kowtowing before two men, whose naked swords plainly intimate the consequences of any attempt to give alarm, or to offer resistance to their demands, have apparently been collecting all the money in the house and are laying it before the thieves. The oblong boxes are iron safes, in which the Japanese keep their money.

From the position of the other members of the gang, it is evident that they have not got all they require, and are watching something going on in the interior of the house. They have probably learnt that the merchant has to forward some money for the purchase of goods by a certain date, and know exactly how much to expect.

In the spring of 1865 the Tycoon, in levying a tax on the Yeddo merchants, congratulated them on the fact that the portion of the country under his immediate control was exempt from the depredations of lonins; but notwithstanding this statement, a robbery of the nature described took place in the capital immediately after the issue of the Tycoon's manifesto, and a lonin concerned in it gave as an excuse for his conduct, that he had learnt that the money was intended for foreigners, who were settled in the country in opposition to the laws of Gongen Sama, which had never been revoked.

With such dread are these men regarded by the non-combatant classes, that it frequently happens that one or two will go into a village and extort what they require without the slightest resistance being offered.

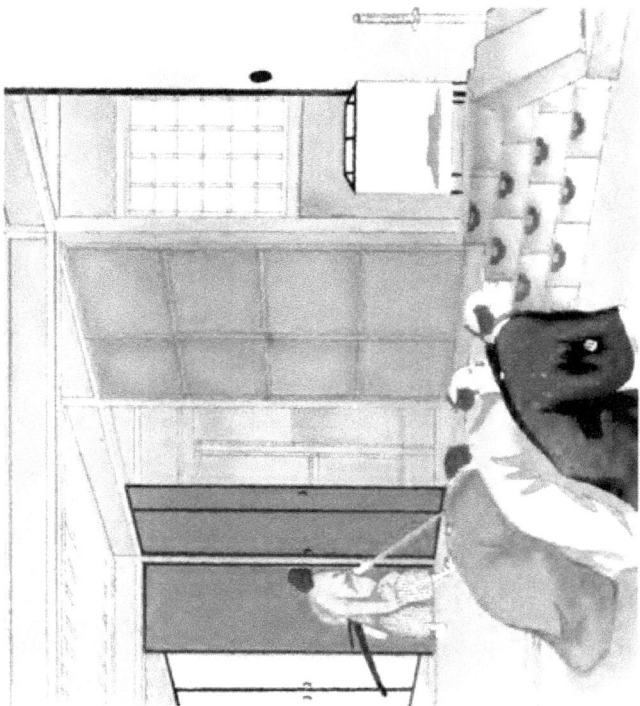

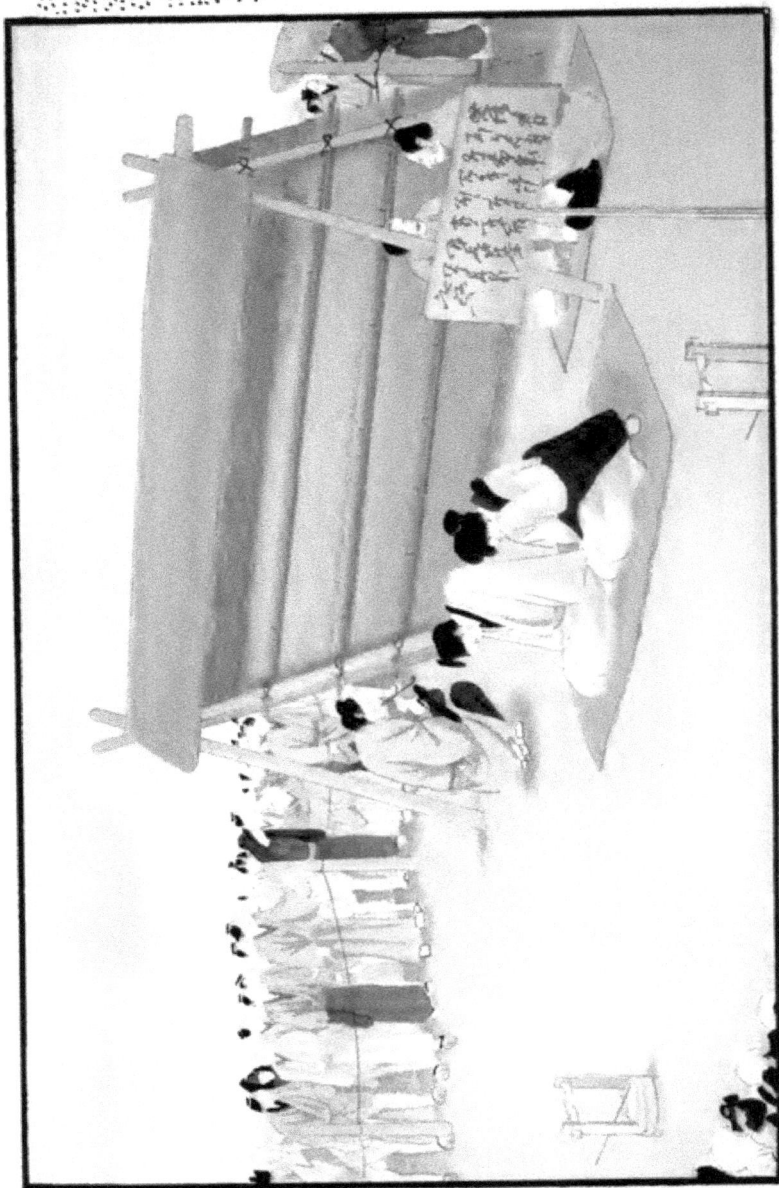

As a rule, Japanese punishments resemble those inflicted by the Chinese, and seem to be based on the Mosaic principle of 'an eye for an eye and a tooth for a tooth.' Arson, for instance. is punished at the stake ; and a thief who endeavours to conceal the results of his robberies by burying them, has the disadvantages of that mode of concealment impressed upon him, by being himself embedded for a day or two in the ground, with only his head out — a mode of instruction that rarely requires a repetition of the lesson.

Apropos of this punishment is the testimony of an eye-witness, who, in passing the public execution place at Yeddo, noticed a head on the ground. which he supposed to have been recently struck off. He had turned away with a shudder, when a laugh from the bystanders caused him to look again, when, to his great astonishment, the head was vigorously puffing at a pipe which the facetious executioner had a few moments before been smoking himself.

The last illustration shows a man and woman undergoing public exposure for adultery—a crime which is rare in Japan, and which is punished with great severity.

With such detestation is it regarded, that, in addition to all legal cognizance, the husband is permitted, in certain instances, to avenge himself by taking the lives of the offenders upon the spot.

The board on the right contains the official intimation of the crime.

The curious instruments depicted in the woodcut are Japanese emblems of justice, and are to be seen at all the guard-houses ; they are used to catch runaway offenders, or to pin a drunken yaconin against a wall or house, and so facilitate the task of disarming him without out danger to the captors.

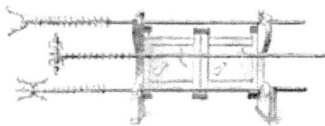

So lleg arami, Sotermate, and Sonobo.

Although the Japanese use torture to extract information from obstinate criminals, they employ all necessary caution to preserve life ; and a doctor and responsible officer are always present when it is employed, as representatives of the respective claims of humanity and justice. A singular punishment, to which only the nobles of the country are liable, is secret banishment to the island of Fatzisiu, which is situated on the northern coast of the empire. It is small and barren, rising perpendicularly from the sea. The only communication with it is by means of a basket, which is lowered from an overhanging tree to the water, a distance of about fifty feet.[*] From this island there is no return, and the unhappy, incarcerated nobles, are compelled to support themselves by weaving silks, which are the most beautiful the country produces. A junk visits the island once a-year, when the silks are exchanged for provisions.

* In 1853 an English man-of-war visited this island, and two of the officers were hoisted up in the basket for the purpose of taking sights. One of them, who was my informant, describes it as a walled-in barren island, with no other mode of ingress or egress than that described.

CHAPTER IX.

THE Sintoo faith and Buddhism are the prevalent religions of the Japanese. The teaching of the other sects is modelled more or less on the tenets inculcated by these two. Some, however, hold a philosophic doctrine, which recognises a Supreme Being but denies a future state, holding that happiness is only to be insured by a virtuous life.

Sintooism may be regarded as the national religion of the country. It inculcates a high moral standard ; and its chief personage is the Mikado, or spiritual emperor, who is considered to be a mediator between his subjects and the inhabitants of the other world.

Every Sintoo has the image of a patron ' kami,' or ' saint,' enshrined in his house, to which he lays open his necessities and confesses his shortcomings, and by whose intercession with the Supreme Being he trusts at his death to be translated to the regions of the ' kamis,' as they designate their heaven.

The wicked are supposed to be consigned to the abodes of the disembodied spirits, who are punished according to the nature of their crimes. For instance, saki merchants who have sold bad spirit are believed to be confined in stagnant pools ; and murderers are supposed to haunt the graves of their victims, until the prayers of their relatives release them. Purity of life and body is the leading feature of the Sintoo faith. As an emblem of the natural purity of the soul, mirrors are hung up in the temples ; and the more ignorant people (who in Japan, like every other country, are most influenced by superstitions) believe, as they look into the mirror, that the Supreme Being sees their past lives as easily as they do their own faces. The value attached to indulgences and charms is very great, and the sale of them contributes largely to the revenues of the Mikado. Charms are eagerly purchased by the lower orders, who carry them about their persons, and never let anybody touch them except themselves.

At a tea-house at Kamakura, one of these charms was accidentally dropped by a lively little 'moosmie,' or 'girl,' who was waiting on a party of foreigners. One of them picked it up, and was on the point of opening the small box in which it is placed for safety when she discovered the loss, and made a desperate rush for its recovery. On finding the importance attached to it, the 'friske,' as she called it, was handed round the group as she eagerly darted after it ; and on one of the party pretending to light a cigar with it she burst into tears, and was not to be pacified until it was restored.

A religious observance of great importance with the Japanese is ' Osurasma,' or ' praying a soul out of purgatory,' as they wisely consider that even the most holy must have some small peccadilloes to answer for.

This ceremony takes place in the seventh month after death : a white lamp is its emblem. This is hung up at the entrance of the mourners' houses, while they offer oblations and burn joss-sticks. Food is also prepared and laid out, in case the spirit of the departed, finding the journey to the regions of the ' kamis ' a long and wearisome one, should need refreshment.

No Japanese dreams of entering a friend's house while the white lamp is hung up, or of disturbing in any way the privacy of a family engaged in these solemn duties, as the spirits of the departed are firmly believed to revisit their former dwellings at such times, if they have not already entered into a state of bliss.

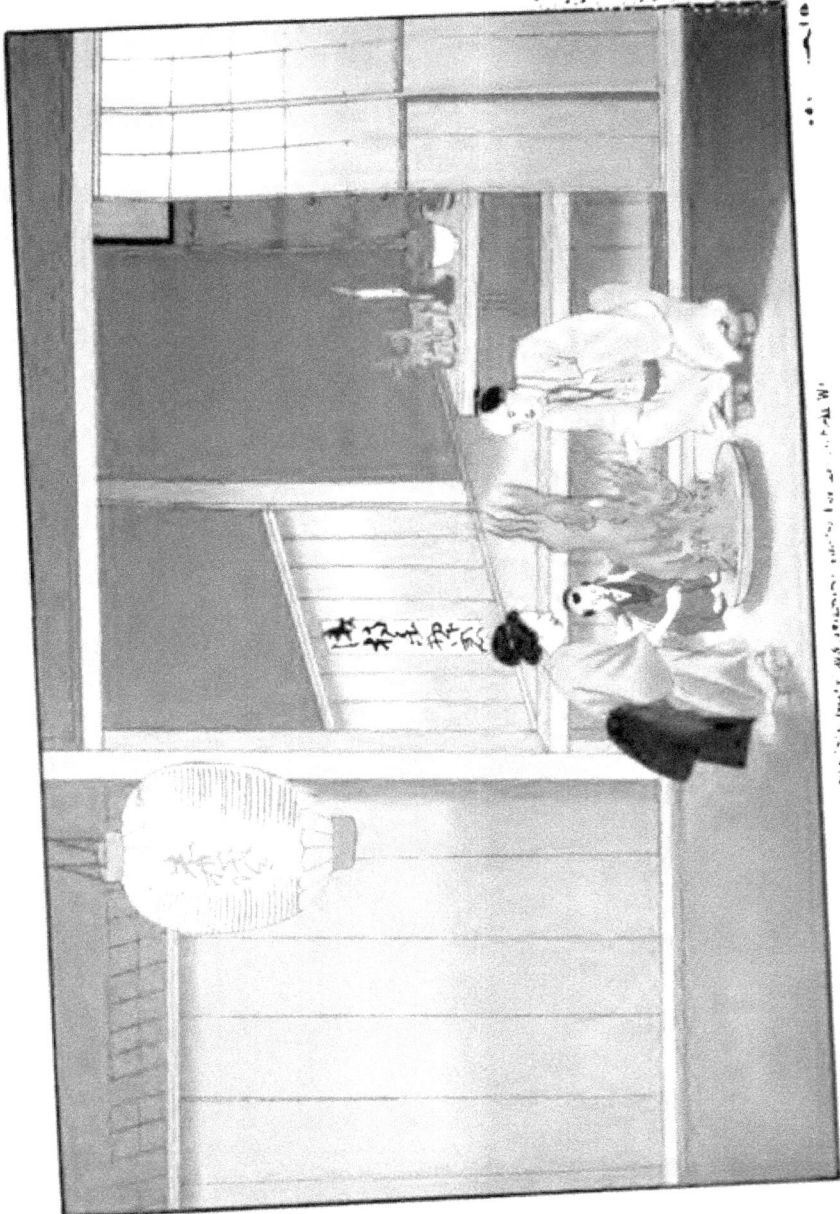

In one of their festivals they make pilgrimages at night to the graves of their friends, on which they place food and hang lamps. It is said they believe their ancestors to come from heaven to them on these occasions, and imagine that they return again in small boats, to which they attach lanterns, and which they place on the water at ebb-tide, on the evening of the last day of the festival, and eagerly watch out of sight. An old fisherman, however, who was observed intently watching his frail bark floating out to sea, explained, on being questioned, that he whose lamp burnt longest caught most fish ; and judging from the old man's solemn manner, there was no doubt he had perfect faith in the truth of his statement.

However gross their superstitions may be, there is no doubt that they affectionately revere the memory of their dead, and treat them with quite as much respect as the most civilised nation in Christendom.

In battle the Japanese always carry off the fallen.

At the bombardment of the Simono-seki forts, at the entrance of the Suwo-Nada, or 'Inland Sea,' in September 1864, Prince Choisiu's loss, according to one of his own officers, amounted to upwards of 500 killed and wounded ; but all had been removed when the brigade of English, French, and Dutch, under the command of Colonel Suther, C.B., Royal Marines, took possession of the forts early next day. At the storming of a stockade (which was pluckily defended) by two battalions of Royal Marines and the light-armed companies of the British squadron, the Japanese were noticed carrying away their dead and wounded, and several were unfortunately shot while thus employed.[*]

A few nights afterwards large fires were noticed in the interior, which were said to be the funeral pyres of those who had fallen in the defence of the forts and stockade.

---

[*] The whole of the operations, with the exception of the storming of the stockade, which took place late in the day after the French and Dutch had embarked, were under the personal superintendence of the English and French admirals.

G

The illustration representing the last offices, depicts a custom of Buddhist origin which is generally adopted by the Japanese. They believe that shaving the head of the dead propitiates the deities in their favour. It is also considered to be an emblem of sanctity, and the bonzes, or priests, always keep their heads clean-shaved. Even children intended for the priesthood, as well as certain religious societies of both sexes, are similarly distinguished. Odder-looking creatures than these bald-headed specimens of humanity can hardly be imagined.

The itinerant sweetmeat vendor shown in the woodcut is a specimen of the class of Japanese most prone to superstition. The lantern he carries serves not only to light his way but to advertise his wares : it also bears his name, no Japanese of the lower orders being allowed to stroll about at night without a lantern so distinguished.

Itinerant Sweetmeat Vendor. [Native Drawing.]

CHAPTER X.

ON THE TOKAIDO AND IN THE TEA-HOUSES.

EXTENDING over the whole empire of Japan, regular ferries connecting it with the different islands, is the 'Tokaido,' or 'Imperial High Road,' to which occasional reference has been made.

Originally constructed at the instigation of a Tycoon of more than ordinary abilities, it has, from the constant care bestowed upon it for centuries (each Daimio being compelled to keep that portion of it which passes through his dominions in repair), become a broad and well-graduated highway.

It is frequently sheltered by avenues of colossal pines, cryptomerias, and other lofty trees; and small plantations of the graceful bamboo are generally to be seen in the neighbourhood of the roadside houses.

The scenery is sometimes very lovely: mountain-ranges are to be observed rising one above another, in that wild conglomeration peculiar to volcanic countries; and in the Island of Nipon the snowy cone of Fusi-yama is almost always visible from the higher ground.

The hilly country is thickly wooded; but terraces of fields are sometimes cut in the sides, where the formation of the ground permits. The lowlands and valleys are mostly covered with rich crops of cereals, which are watered by natural or artificial streams.

As the Tokaido winds along the hill-tops, occasional glimpses of the sea meet the eye, often with a series of headlands jutting one beyond another into it, and distant islands dotting the horizon.

By the wayside many rare and beautiful ferns are to be seen ; and in their seasons, the large white lilies of the country, hydrangeas, violets, orchids, and an endless variety of wild flowers.

Along this beautiful road are constantly passing Daimios and their hosts of retainers, trains of travellers and pilgrims, and a large portion of the inland traffic of the empire. As the Tokaido passes through most of the principal towns, the traveller has frequent opportunities of observing the various avocations of the people; for mechanics commonly work in front of their doors, as shown in the woodcut : and in fine weather, the sliding windows through which the Japanese enter their houses are always drawn back, leaving the interior and its occupants open to the road.

The baker's shop opposite affords a good specimen of the wayside scenes, and conveys a fair idea of an ordinary Japanese house. It will be noticed that the puppies in the foreground, as well as the cat in the girl's arms, are very indifferently delineated ; but such animals are the especial stumbling-blocks of the native artists, although they faithfully represent birds, fishes, and reptiles.

Carpenters at work. [Native Drawing.]

With the exception of the Daimios on their state journeys (who, by the way, have regular halting-places at tea-houses officially set apart for their use), the mass of the people to be seen on the Tokaido belong to the lower classes — the aristocracy considering it beneath their dignity to travel for pleasure, or to make pilgrimages.

Naturally hardy and energetic, the Japanese seem thoroughly to enjoy travelling, which in fine weather has few drawbacks. It is true that the peremptory order, 'Chetanerio,' or 'Down upon your knees,' at the approach of one of their oligarchical rulers, would be objectionable to Europeans ; but the Japanese are accustomed to this, and proceed with their journey after half-an-hour's detention without being in any way put out by it.

The numerous and pleasant tea-houses that skirt the Tokaido have a great deal to do with rendering travelling popular. A smiling welcome from the pretty waitresses employed at these places may always be anticipated by the weary wayfarers ; and, however slight their requirements may be, they are certain to be promptly and courteously attended to.

If the means of travellers do not permit them to resort to the tea-houses, there are sheds and stalls at intervals along the road, where they can obtain fruit or refreshments at a trifling cost.

Some of the tea-houses in the vicinity

Tea-house Girl waiting. [Nature Drawing.]

of large towns are much frequented in the spring-time by pleasure-parties, on account of the beauty of their gardens. The chromo-lithograph opposite represents one of these parties, some of whom appear to have been indulging too freely in saki. The fellow dancing and waving the fan about is apparently addressing a love-song to the lady opposite, whose husband is evidently desirous of putting a stop to the flirtation.

CHAPTER XI.

THE SPY SYSTEM—THE BATH-HOUSE.

THERE are two Japanese customs so diametrically opposed to English ideas, and so materially affecting the national character, that it is necessary to call special attention to them.

The espionage system is perhaps the strangest, as every one in the country is subjected to it, from the Mikado and Tycoon, or spiritual and temporal emperors, to the humblest of the people.

All offices of importance are double ; that is to say, every governor of a town or district is associated with a vice-governor, who is an 'ometsky,' or 'spy,' upon him, and is in turn spied upon by others. In this way a constant check is kept upon the executive of the empire.

In addition to this acknowledged system, government officials are frequently watched by secret spies, who, for aught they know, may be some apparently trusty friend : so that, even in the absence of their double, they can never be certain that they are free from supervision.

In private life families spy on each other, for which purpose they are divided into coteries of five households, the heads of which are not only responsible for themselves, their families and servants, but also for the other members of the coterie ; and any wrong-doing in one household must be immediately reported to the proper authorities, to secure the rest from sharing in the punishment of the offence.

To such an extent is this system of responsibility carried, that a whole

district sometimes suffers for the offence of one of its residents. In the towns, where the streets are intersected with barriers a few hundred yards apart, which are always closed at night, the people living within these enclosures are often under the ban of the officials for some irregularity which has occurred within the limits. This constant espionage has, of course, a very pernicious effect upon the character of the people, as it necessarily instils feelings of distrust and suspicion among near neighbours. Yet it is marvellous how well their social system works, and still more marvellous that the officials, who in public life practise every kind of deception and artifice, should be, and from all accounts deservedly so, distinguished in private life for their truthfulness, candour, and hospitality.

The other notable peculiarity is the indiscriminate manner in which the sexes mingle in the public bath-houses. All Japanese perform their ablutions once or twice a-day; for which purpose the poorer classes resort to the bath-houses, which are generally open to the road or street.

Some bath-houses have the women's lavatory separate; and one of these is the subject of the illustration. This arrangement, however, is more for convenience than in compliance with the demands of modesty as is evidenced by the fact that a male attendant is supplying water; and that his presence is plainly a matter of perfect indifference to the women bathing, with their children, in his immediate vicinity.

But it is in the common bath-room where this extraordinary feature of Japanese life unmistakeably presents itself. There men, women and children, perform their ablutions together, with all the apparent innocency of our first parents. The proceedings are conducted with perfect order and good-nature. The steaming occupants make way for one another with ball-room politeness; they laugh and chat over their tubs, discuss the public notices on the walls, or, maybe, saunter occasionally to the open door or window, to look at something which has attracted their attention, or to exchange greetings with a passing friend. All this is done with a freedom that speaks for itself of their utter unconsciousness of any impropriety in their conduct.

the skill of the artist, the other branches having been lopped off, or stunted, to facilitate the growth and training of this one.

Gardens for the sale of dwarf trees and flowers are also very common. Some are perfect *bijoux.* As a rule the varied collections of flowers, planted in coloured china pots, are arranged, with very agreeable effect, in tiers of shelves round the sides, and on stands about the gardens.

Many of the dwarf trees, especially the maples, have great variety of foliage, the result of constant grafting. To such an extent is this practised, that it is rare to find pure botanical specimens in a Japanese garden.

Plants are sometimes cultivated for their berries as well as for their variegated foliage. One very beautiful specimen, producing at the same time bright scarlet and yellow berries, is believed by many to have been obtained from cuttings of an exquisite shrub, which is said to be the principal ornament of the regions of the ' Kamis,' or Japanese heaven.

Even the fern family undergoes a strange metamorphosis at the hands of Japanese gardeners. Some of the fronds are artificially variegated ; and others, on reaching maturity, have a curious crumpled appearance. Again, the roots of certain small species are frequently twisted into curious devices, and hung up in grottoes, or shady corners. The effect of these, when the roots are partly concealed by the fresh young fronds, is very pretty.

Nearly every fortnight a fresh flower comes into season, and is in great demand for the time ; heavy prices being readily paid for fine specimens.

The poorer classes commonly buy flowers from men who gain their livelihood by hawking them about the streets. They buy them not only to gratify their tastes, but as offerings to their Lares and Penates— patron ' Kamis ;' or to decorate the tombs of departed relatives—a religious ceremony which is strictly observed.

Flower-shows are often held in the large towns, and are much frequented by the people.

The illustration represents a chrysanthemum show. These flowers are much esteemed by the Japanese, who pay more attention to size and brilliancy of colour than to perfume. The stone in the centre is called a 'skakeshe.' On it, poetry in praise of flowers is inscribed. This is a custom of very ancient origin, and poetical inscriptions on stones and rocks are to be often seen in public places. The piece of ornamental stonework is an 'ishedoro,' or 'stone lamp;' which is very common in gardens, and is much prized on account of the historical associations connected with it.

The Japanese have many floral compliments. A very pretty one is intimated by a present of seeds (especially if presented to a foreigner returning to his own country), the purport being,—'Plant these seeds about your home, and, when you see them growing, think of me.'

As an instance of the influence which flowers have upon the Japanese character, the word 'hanna,' or flower, is commonly used as a term of endearment: it is usually applied by parents to a favourite daughter, or by a lover to his mistress; it is also used to distinguish the bride and the bridegroom, as 'hanna-yomie,' 'hanna-moko.' Floral love-tokens (although they only consist of a single sprig) are as much prized among the Japanese as among ourselves; and are, no doubt, sometimes

Girl with Flowers.

" Treasured in their fading,"

as the Japanese are not only poetical, but much given to sentimental reflections.

LONDON:
DAY AND SON, LIMITED.
GATE STREET LINCOLN'S INN FIELDS.

www.ingramcontent.com/pod-product-compliance
Lightning Source LLC
Chambersburg PA
CBHW030539270326
41927CB00008B/1441